ECO-DISASTERS

OIL SPILL

DEEPWATER HORIZON

by Meish Goldish

Consultant: Samantha Joye
Oceanographer
University of Georgia
Athens, Georgia

BEARPORT
PUBLISHING

New York, New York

Credits

Cover and Title Page, © Reuters/Alamy; 5, © USCG/PSG/Newscom; 7T, © REUTERS/Alamy; 7B, © AP Photo/Dave Martin; 8, © AP Photo/Janet McConnaughey; 9T, The Design Lab; 9B, © AP Photo/Dave Martin; 10, © JOHN FITZHUGH/MCT/Newscom; 11, © AP Photo/Eric Gay; 12T, © You Touch Pix of EuToch/Shutterstock; 12B, © All Canada Photos/Alamy; 13, © beltsazar/Shutterstock; 14, © AP Photo/Gerald Herbert; 15T, © AP Photo/Charlie Riedel; 15B, © LARRY W. SMITH/EPA/Newscom; 16, © AP Photo/Charlie Riedel; 17, © AP Photo/Cain Burdeau; 18, Courtesy of the US Coast Guard; 19, © Cp John Masson/ZUMA Press/Newscom; 20, © AP Photo/Patrick Semansky; 21L, © Mati Nitibhon/Shutterstock; 21R, © Nature Photographers Ltd/Alamy; 22, © Reuters/Alamy; 23L, © AP Photo/Dave Martin; 23R, © ANN HEISENFELT/EPA/Newscom; 24T, © DAN ANDERSON/EPA/Newscom; 24B, © Reuters/Alamy; 25, © Peter Leahy/Shutterstock; 26, © Clifford Rhodes/Alamy; 27, © Prentice Danner/ZUMApress/Newscom; 28L, © AP Photo/Manuel Balce Ceneta; 28R, © W. Scott McGill/Shutterstock; 29T, © Tetra Images/Alamy; 29B, © Cheryl Casey/Shutterstock; 31, © beltsazar/Shutterstock.

Publisher: Kenn Goin
Editor: Jessica Rudolph
Creative Director: Spencer Brinker
Photo Researcher: Editorial Directions, Inc.

Library of Congress Cataloging-in-Publication Data

Names: Goldish, Meish, author.
Title: Oil spill : Deepwater Horizon / by Meish Goldish.
Description: New York, New York : Bearport Publishing, 2018. | Series:
   Eco-disasters | Audience: Ages 5 to 8. | Includes bibliographical
   references and index.
Identifiers: LCCN 2017007442 (print) | LCCN 2017012481 (ebook) |
ISBN 9781684022809 (ebook) | ISBN 9781684022267 (library bound)
Subjects: LCSH: BP Deepwater Horizon Explosion and Oil Spill, 2010—Juvenile
   literature. | Oil spills—Mexico, Gulf of—History—21st century—Juvenile
   literature. | Oil spills—Environmental aspects—Mexico, Gulf
   of—History—21st century—Juvenile literature. | Oil wells—Mexico, Gulf
   of—Blowouts—History—21st century—Juvenile literature.
Classification: LCC TD427.P4 (ebook) | LCC TD427.P4 G59 2018 (print) | DDC
   363.11/9622338190916364—dc23
LC record available at https://lccn.loc.gov/2017007442

For more information, write to Bearport Publishing Company, Inc., 45 West 21st Street, Suite 3B, New York, New York 10010. Printed in the United States of America.

10 9 8 7 6 5 4 3 2 1

Contents

Fire!

The worst day of Stephen Davis's life was on April 20, 2010. He and 125 other men and women were working on an **oil rig** in the **Gulf** of Mexico. The rig, called Deepwater Horizon, was drilling for oil that lay deep beneath the ocean floor. Suddenly, a gas leak caused a huge explosion and a terrible fire. Davis remembered the giant blast. "The whole rig was shaking. . . . You could taste the **fumes**. It was hard to breathe."

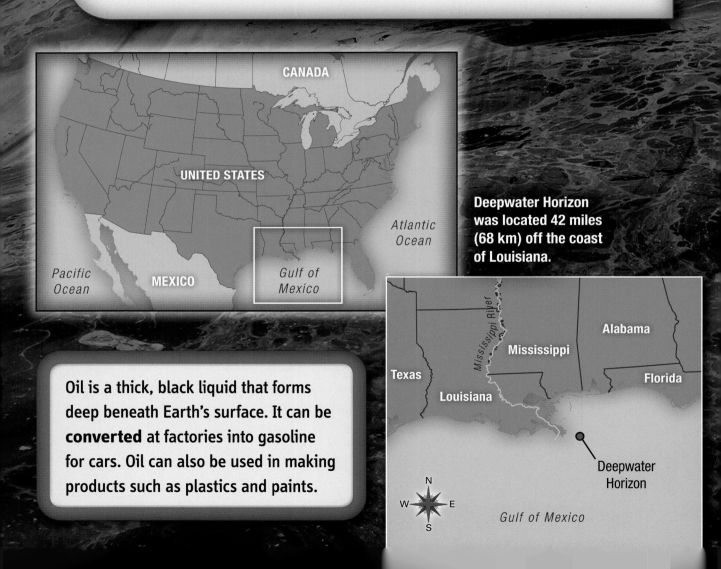

Deepwater Horizon was located 42 miles (68 km) off the coast of Louisiana.

Oil is a thick, black liquid that forms deep beneath Earth's surface. It can be **converted** at factories into gasoline for cars. Oil can also be used in making products such as plastics and paints.

After the explosion, most of the workers quickly escaped in lifeboats. Some jumped into the ocean and were saved by nearby rescue boats. Sadly, 11 workers were killed by the blast.

The U.S. **Coast Guard** sent fireboats to the scene, but they were unable to put out the gigantic flames. After burning for 36 hours, the huge oil rig finally sank 5,000 feet (1,524 m) to the bottom of the ocean.

Fireboats tried to put out flames that rose as high as a 15-story building.

A Second Disaster

Two days after Deepwater Horizon sank, the Coast Guard discovered an **oil slick** on the water's surface. It stretched for 5 miles (8 km) across the Gulf. The oil came from a long pipe that connected the rig to an underground well. The pipe had cracked during the explosion. Now, hundreds of thousands of gallons of oil were gushing from the broken pipe into the ocean.

How an Oil Rig Works

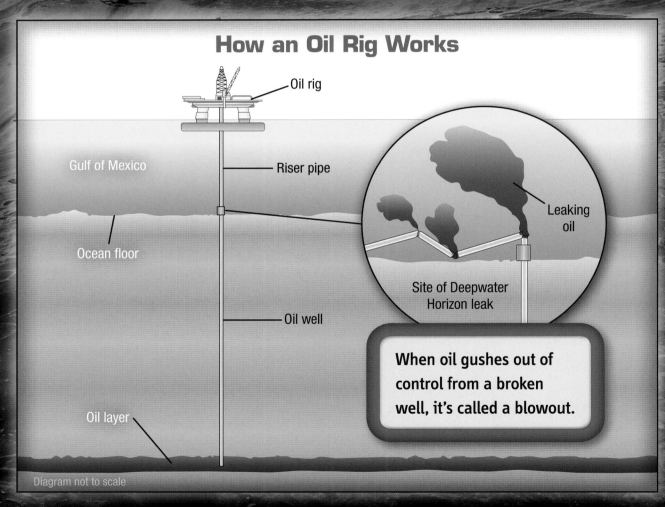

Oil rig

Gulf of Mexico

Riser pipe

Ocean floor

Leaking oil

Site of Deepwater Horizon leak

Oil well

When oil gushes out of control from a broken well, it's called a blowout.

Oil layer

Diagram not to scale

On an oil rig, a riser pipe carries oil from the underground well up to the rig. When Deepwater Horizon exploded, the oil started leaking about 1 mile (1.6 km) below the ocean's surface.

The broken pipe needed to be repaired—and fast! Otherwise, oil would keep spilling into the water. The oil could do serious harm to ocean animals and plants. U.S. Coast Guard Rear Admiral Mary Landry said, "If we don't secure the well, this could be one of the most significant oil spills in U.S. history."

U.S. Coast Guard Rear Admiral Mary Landry

The oil slick turned the Gulf's greenish-blue waters reddish-brown.

Racing Against Time

Fixing the broken pipe would not be easy. The water **pressure** 1 mile (1.6 km) under the ocean's surface made it impossible for people to safely work there. Instead, remote-controlled underwater robots were used to collect information about the exact location of the leak and then try to repair the pipe. However, their efforts to repair it failed because the rush of oil was simply too powerful.

GORDON GUNTER
IMO 8835255

On May 28, 2010, a U.S. government research ship lowered a robot submarine called the Gulper into the ocean to gather information about the oil spill.

An oil company named BP was responsible for fixing the broken pipe, since it owned the oil well in the Gulf and had been paying a company called TransOcean to operate the rig.

Day after day, more oil spilled into the ocean. By May, the slick had grown to almost 4,000 square miles (10,400 sq km)—three times the size of Rhode Island! Strong winds blew the oil toward the southern U.S. coast. In early June, oil reached the shores of Louisiana, Mississippi, and Alabama. By July, **tar balls** were found on beaches in Florida. Scientists worried that the ocean **current** might carry the oil up the eastern U.S. seacoast. How far would this oily monster spread—and could it be stopped?

The extent of the BP oil spill by July 2010

Tar balls from the BP spill on a beach in Alabama

One Win, Many Losses

On July 15, almost three full months after the explosion, robots finally managed to place a **cement** cap on the leaking oil pipe. At last, the oil flow stopped. By that time, however, 206 million gallons (780 million liters) of oil had poured into the ocean! It was now **polluting** the Gulf waters and the Gulf States' coastlines.

Workers remove tar balls from a polluted Mississippi beach.

Thousands of ocean animals died from the oil spill, including fish, birds, sea turtles, and whales. Oil covered their bodies, making it impossible for them to move, eat, or breathe. Thousands of other animals were still alive but needed help immediately. Workers had two important jobs to do. One was to rescue the animals at risk. The other was to clean up the oily mess in the ocean and on the beaches.

A dead crab lies on an oil-covered beach in Louisiana.

Shortly after the oil spill began, President Barack Obama formed a National Response Team made up of 16 government departments. Together, they organized a Gulf cleanup that included rescuing animals and collecting oil.

Saving Eggs

Months before the oil flow was stopped, a large animal rescue had already begun for sea turtles. In the spring, female turtles had laid their eggs on sandy beaches along the southern U.S. coast. When the eggs hatched in the summer, the baby turtles would swim into oily waters that would kill them.

Kemp's ridley sea turtles live in the Gulf of Mexico.

Many types of sea turtles dig nests on the beach, lay their eggs, and then cover them with sand. The eggs hatch

All along the southern U.S. coast, **volunteers**—guided by **veterinarians**—dug up turtle nests that held thousands of eggs. They carefully packed each egg in sand. The eggs were then sent to a part of Florida where the oil had not reached the shores and where the waters were clear. The ocean water there was clean and safe for the newborn turtles.

A newly hatched baby sea turtle crawls toward the ocean on a Florida beach.

Bird Baths

Rescuers worked hard to save many other animals that were harmed by the oil spill, including seabirds. Gerald Herbert, a writer and photographer, saw the damaging effects on pelicans, herons, egrets, and other birds up close. He wrote, "It was quite a horror show. Birds were swimming in oiled water." The birds that clung to life needed to be cleaned before the oil killed them.

This oil-covered bird is stuck to the side of a ship.

Workers collected the **fragile** creatures from the ocean waters and beaches. Then they gently washed the birds with liquid soap and water to remove oil from their feathers. They fed the birds and kept them in outdoor pools until they were strong enough to live on their own. Once a doctor decided that a bird was healthy, it was set free.

Workers carefully clean a pelican covered in oil.

The Smithsonian National Zoological Park was one group that taught volunteers how to rescue and clean birds.

Workers feed a rescued seabird.

Too Late for Some

Sadly, not all oil spill **victims** were able to be rescued in time. Many sea turtles died after eating globs of oil, thinking they might have been jellyfish. Seabirds **perished** when oil got into their throats and stomachs and on their feathers. They were unable to breathe, keep warm, or fly.

This sea turtle was a victim of the oil spill.

The Deepwater Horizon disaster was the largest oil spill in U.S. history.

Even animals that lived deep in the ocean were affected. That's because some of the oil settled down near the ocean floor. Many sharks, dolphins, and whales that swam in the deep waters breathed the oil and died. Others died after eating fish that were already **poisoned** by the oil.

Many dead dolphins washed up on beaches.

Collecting and Burning

Trying to rescue sea animals was one important job after the oil spill. The other was cleaning up the millions of gallons of oil that polluted the ocean waters and shores. In some areas, workers in boats placed long floating **barriers**, called booms, around the oil on the water's surface to keep the oil from spreading farther.

skimmer

boom

With booms in place, workers use skimmers to collect the oil.

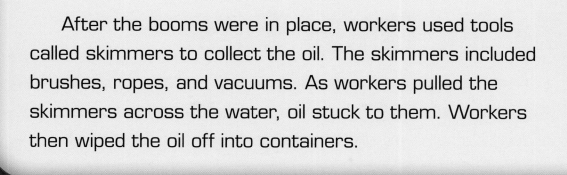

After the booms were in place, workers used tools called skimmers to collect the oil. The skimmers included brushes, ropes, and vacuums. As workers pulled the skimmers across the water, oil stuck to them. Workers then wiped the oil off into containers.

In ocean areas that were farther from animal habitats, workers set fires to burn the oil off the ocean's surface. Although the fires got rid of the oil, the smoke they produced polluted the air.

Making Things Worse

Another way that workers got rid of spilled oil was by using chemicals called dispersants. Planes and helicopters sprayed dispersants on the oil slick. The chemicals were also pumped underwater where the oil had erupted from the sea floor. The dispersants broke up the oil into tiny drops. Some of the oil drops were then eaten by **bacteria** in the water.

An airplane sprays dispersants on the oil slick in the Gulf.

The dispersants did the job of breaking up the oil into tiny drops. Yet they also caused problems. The poisonous chemicals harmed tiny ocean plants and animals called **plankton**. Small sea animals such as shrimp depend on plankton for food. As a result, many of these animals in the Gulf died. Later, larger fish and other sea animals died, too, because they depended on the smaller animals for food. The dispersants had affected the entire ocean **food chain**.

Some of the dispersants used in the BP oil spill had been **banned** in England because they were considered too harmful to ocean life. The U.S. government approved the chemicals, however, hoping they would stop the oil slick from reaching land.

A shrimp

A close-up photograph of plankton

Harm to Workers

The BP oil spill harmed more than just sea plants and animals. It also affected thousands of workers in businesses that depend on the ocean. For example, many areas of the Gulf that were polluted were closed off to fishers. These people, who usually caught and sold tuna, sharks, oysters, and shrimp for food, suddenly had no work.

People who worked in beach towns were also hurt by the spill. Swimming and other beach activities were now unsafe, so many beaches had to close. Workers in hotels and shops were soon out of jobs. Lifeguards and other beach workers also became unemployed. Even where beaches stayed open, few visitors showed up.

SWIMMING WATER QUALITY STATUS
HEALTH ADVISORY:

THE PUBLIC IS ADVISED NOT TO SWIM IN THESE WATERS DUE TO THE PRESENCE OF OIL-RELATED CHEMICALS

For More Information:
Alabama Dept. Of Public Health
www.adph.org

BEACH CLOSED

In Grand Isle, Louisiana, during the summer of 2010, the number of visitors dropped from the usual 10,000 to only about 100.

A warning sign at an Alabama beach

Paying for Damages

Because of the huge amount of damage caused by the spill, the U.S. government decided to sue BP. It claimed that the oil company had operated Deepwater Horizon in a careless manner. In 2012, BP pled guilty to **felony** charges and agreed to pay $4 billion in fines.

Some of the BP money was used to pay thousands of workers who cleaned up the beaches and ocean.

Most of the BP money was used to **restore** the ocean and beaches, including **coral reefs** close to shore and in deep waters that the oil had destroyed. Reefs are home to many sea animals, such as oysters. They provide food for birds, fish, and crabs. Reefs also stop ocean waves from **eroding** the shore.

A coral reef off the coast of Florida

During the cleanup, workers planted **artificial** reefs to create new homes for sea creatures.

Studying the Effects

Today, the effects of the BP oil spill are still being felt. More than 1,000 miles (1,609 km) of shoreline, from Texas to Florida, were touched by the disaster. Some southern coastal land has even disappeared. How? Ocean waves erode the land where coral reefs once held back the water. Less land has led to fewer homes for seabirds and other coastal animals.

Between 2010 and 2016, about 700,000 birds died of illnesses or injuries caused by the oil spill.

The oil spill also affected life deep in the ocean. After the well was capped, scientists discovered oil up to 4 inches (10 cm) thick on the ocean floor. How will that oil affect ocean life in years to come? Scientists aren't sure yet. They do agree on one thing, however. People must find ways to avoid harmful oil spills in the future, so that ocean waters will stay clean and safe.

A cleanup worker picks up tar balls on a beach in Texas that will be sent to a lab and analyzed.

In 2010, the National Institute of Health began a ten-year study of 33,000 cleanup workers and volunteers at spill sites. Doctors want to find out if the workers' **exposure** to the oil and dispersants is affecting their health.

Fixing the Future

Since the Deepwater Horizon disaster of 2010, actions have been taken to try to prevent more oil spills from occurring in the future. Here are some examples.

Talking to Congress

In 2010, Dr. Sylvia Earle, an environmental expert, spoke before the U.S. Congress. She urged lawmakers to more closely oversee the practices used for drilling oil in the ocean. Other experts called for less ocean oil drilling.

Dr. Sylvia Earle

Wind turbines on a wind farm

Other Forms of Energy

Many experts have encouraged the U.S. government to focus on other forms of energy—such as solar and wind—to meet the nation's future needs. This type of energy, called clean energy, creates less pollution than oil, coal, and gas.

Safety Changes

In 2011, BP changed its safety practices for drilling oil in the ocean. One change was to use a more reliable type of cement cap that would shut down an out-of-control oil well in less time. Another change was to use new equipment that would cut through damaged oil pipes and make repairs faster on a broken well.

Oil rig workers

New Rules

In 2016, the U.S. Congress passed its own set of safety rules for oil companies regarding the capping of oil wells and preventing oil rig explosions. The rules include closer inspections of equipment used on oil rigs.

More Payments

According to the terms of its legal agreement, BP continued to spend more money to restore the Gulf. As of 2015, the company had spent more than $28 billion on cleanups, repairs, and payments to spill victims for loss of work.

Oil cleanup workers

Glossary

artificial (ar-tih-FISH-uhl) made by human beings

bacteria (bac-TEER-ee-uh) tiny life forms that can be seen only under a microscope

banned (BAND) not allowed to be used

barriers (BA-ree-urz) things that block the way

cement (suh-MENT) a gray powder that becomes hard when mixed with water and left to dry

coast guard (KOHST GARD) a branch of the military that protects a nation's coasts and comes to the aid of boats and ships in trouble

converted (kuhn-VUR-tid) changed from one substance, form, or use to another

coral reefs (KORE-uhl REEFS) rock-like structures formed from the skeletons of sea animals called coral polyps

current (KUR-uhnt) the movement of water in an ocean or river

eroding (ih-ROHD-ing) gradually wearing away by water or wind

exposure (eks-POH-shur) the state of being in contact with something dangerous

felony (FEL-uh-nee) a serious crime punishable by a heavy sentence

food chain (FOOD CHAYN) a series of plants and animals that depend on one another for food

fragile (FRAJ-il) weak; easily hurt

fumes (FYOOMZ) gas or smoke given off by chemicals or something that is burning

gulf (GULF) a part of an ocean or sea partially surrounded by land

oil rig (OYL RIG) a platform used to drill for oil beneath the ocean floor

oil slick (OYL SLIK) a layer of oil floating on the surface of the water

perished (PAIR-ishd) died

plankton (PLANGK-tuhn) tiny animals and plants that float in oceans and lakes

poisoned (POI-zuhnd) made sick or killed by a harmful substance

polluting (puh-LOOT-ing) damaging the air, water, or land with harmful materials

pressure (PRESH-ur) the force made by pressing on something

restore (rih-STORE) to bring something back to its original condition

tar balls (TAHR BAWLZ) lumps of oil

veterinarians (*vet*-ur-uh-NAIR-ee-uhnz) doctors who treat sick and injured animals

victims (VIK-tuhmz) people or animals who are hurt, injured, or killed by something or someone

volunteers (vol-uhn-TEERZ) people who help others for free

Bibliography

Cavnar, Bob. *Disaster on the Horizon: High Stakes, High Risks, and the Story Behind the Deepwater Well Blowout.* White River Junction, VT: Chelsea Green (2011).

Jacobs, Daniel. *BP Blowout: Inside the Gulf Oil Disaster.* Washington, DC: Brookings Institution Press (2016).

Lustgarten, Abrahm. *Run to Failure: BP and the Making of the Deepwater Horizon Disaster.* New York: W.W. Norton (2012).

Read More

Beech, Linda Ward. *The* Exxon Valdez's *Deadly Oil Spill (Code Red).* New York: Bearport (2007).

Benoit, Peter. *The BP Oil Spill (A True Book).* New York: Scholastic (2011).

Landau, Elaine. *Oil Spill! Disaster in the Gulf of Mexico.* Minneapolis, MN: Millbrook Press (2011).

Person, Stephen. *Saving Animals from Oil Spills (Rescuing Animals from Disasters).* New York: Bearport (2012).

Learn More Online

To learn more about the Deepwater Horizon oil spill, visit
www.bearportpublishing.com/EcoDisasters

Index

About the Author

Meish Goldish has written more than 300 books for children. His book *City Firefighters* won a Teachers' Choice Award in 2015. He lives in Brooklyn, New York.